DEVELOP
LOGICAL REASONING

Jean Gilliam DeGaetano

Illustrated by Kevin M. Newman

Great Ideas for Teaching, Inc. • **P.O. Box 444** • **Wrightsville Beach, NC 28480**

ISBN 1-886143-45-5

DEVELOPING LOGICAL REASONING

By Jean Gilliam DeGaetano
Illustrations by Kevin M. Newman

Designed for ages 6-9

This unit is designed to provide questions that develop logical reasoning skills and improve the ability to verbally express logical answers.

At a very early age, children want to know "WHY" about everything. It is a natural process of developing reasoning skills and storing vast information about the reason things happen, the reason things are as they are, and the reason certain things happen as a result of a particular action.

While the majority of children can answer "What would you do?" questions without difficulty, other children who are experiencing a delay in developing language skills need structured practice in developing logical reasoning skills and in expressing their thoughts about what should be done or what would likely be done or would happen in particular situations.

To use the unit successfully, the children should be able to speak in short sentences. Their grammar does not need to be perfect; although the professional should model correct grammar when repeating the children's sentences.

At first, the professional may not have an accurate determination of the depth of the child's reasoning skills, but as the child develops the ability to express his/her thoughts in short sentences and has the vocabulary to do so, the ability to reason and use logic will become apparent when progressing through the unit.

Children with word retrieval problems usually experience more difficulty on nouns. Giving answers to the questions in this unit primarily incorporates pronouns and action words, with the nouns falling at the end of the sentences. Nouns at the end of the sentences usually make retrieval easier since the first part of the sentence signals or provides the association needed to retrieve the appropriate word.

Directions:

Make copies of the masters ahead of time and file for convenient use. A student page should be given to each child. The professional will use the instructional guide page that matches the children's pages.

1. For each picture, the professional reads the statement and question. One child should answer both questions while the other children listen.

2. Next, address another child. Look at the picture and ask that child what the person or animal in the picture is doing. The second child's response should be similar to what was previously said. If it isn't, reread the sentence. Then once again, read the questions to be answered by the second child. Answering again increases the chances of the children retaining the information. Continue in this way until the page is completed.

3. For children who are having difficulty, reviewing some of the pages will be beneficial.

Instructor's Worksheet

Directions: Before beginning, each student should be given a copy of the page that corresponds to the instructor's worksheet. The students are to look at each picture while the instructor reads the statement and questions aloud. One student answers a question (taking turns). The other students can be asked if they agree. If an answer needs to be expanded, the instructor should ask the child additional questions so that the final result is a logical answer.

The girl is getting ready to go to bed.

1. What will she probably do next?

2. Do you think she will be cold tonight? Why or why not?

The girl is putting on her shirt and skirt to go to school.

1. What will she probably do next?

2. Is it daytime or nighttime? How do you know?

The boy splashed the milk on the table.

1. What should he do?

2. Will he still have a mess? Why not?

The boy does not want the toothpaste to leak out of the tube.

1. What should he do?

2. If the cap is on the table, can the toothpaste leak out?

Instructor's Worksheet

Directions: Before beginning, each student should be given a copy of the page that corresponds to the instructor's worksheet. The students are to look at each picture while the instructor reads the statement and questions aloud. One student answers a question (taking turns). The other students can be asked if they agree. If an answer needs to be expanded, the instructor should ask the child additional questions so that the final result is a logical answer.

The girl wants to make a paper heart.

1. What will she probably do next?

2. Then what should she do with the scissors? Why?

The windows are dirty.

1. What should the girl do?

2. Will they ever get dirty again?

The clothes on the clothesline are dry.

1. What should the mother do next?

2. What will she do after she takes the clothes off the clothesline?

The dishes are wet.

1. What will the girl do next?

2. What will she do with the dry dishes?

Instructor's Worksheet

Directions: Before beginning, each student should be given a copy of the page that corresponds to the instructor's worksheet. The students are to look at each picture while the instructor reads the statement and questions aloud. One student answers a question (taking turns). The other students can be asked if they agree. If an answer needs to be expanded, the instructor should ask the child additional questions so that the final result is a logical answer.

The man stuck his finger on a rose thorn and made it bleed.

1. What will he probably do next?

2. What should you do to keep from getting stuck on thorns?

The boy sees a red light.

1. What should he do?

2. Why will it be hard for him to stop quickly?

The baby is sleepy.

1. What should the father do?

2. Do you think the baby will play in its bed or go to sleep? Why?

The boy wants to stop flying his kite.

1. What should he do?

2. What makes a kite fly?

Instructor's Worksheet

Directions: Before beginning, each student should be given a copy of the page that corresponds to the instructor's worksheet. The students are to look at each picture while the instructor reads the statement and questions aloud. One student answers a question (taking turns). The other students can be asked if they agree. If an answer needs to be expanded, the instructor should ask the child additional questions so that the final result is a logical answer.

The girl wants her picture to be in bright colors.

1. What colors should she use?

2. Would a picture be bright if you colored it black?

The man wants to win the race.

1. What should he do?

2. Why do slow runners not win races?

The football player wants the ball to go very far.

1. What should he do?

2. Why is he using a ball holder?

The boy's shoestring broke.

1. What should he do?

2. What happens to your shoe when the shoestring breaks?

Name: _____

Instructor's Worksheet

Directions: Before beginning, each student should be given a copy of the page that corresponds to the instructor's worksheet. The students are to look at each picture while the instructor reads the statement and questions aloud. One student answers a question (taking turns). The other students can be asked if they agree. If an answer needs to be expanded, the instructor should ask the child additional questions so that the final result is a logical answer.

The girl's friend just left and went out the door.

1. What should the girl do to the door?

2. Why should people not leave their doors open?

The boy wants to sit on one of the tree limbs.

1. What should he do?

2. Why is it probably safe to sit on one of the big limbs?

The hole for the tree is too small.

1. What should the man do?

2. What will he probably do after he puts the tree in the hole?

The man wants to stop water skiing.

1. What should he do?

2. Will he get wet? Why?

Name: _____

Instructor's Worksheet

Directions: Before beginning, each student should be given a copy of the page that corresponds to the instructor's worksheet. The students are to look at each picture while the instructor reads the questions aloud. One student answers a question (taking turns). The other students can be asked if they agree. If an answer needs to be expanded, the instructor should ask the child additional questions so that the final result is a logical answer.

1. If the ice starts to melt, what should the boy do?

2. Why can't people skate on thin ice?

1. If the boy does not want to fall off the sled, what should he do?

2. Why do sleds slide fast on hills?

1. When the man sees the goat running after him, what should he do?

2. Why should the man have stayed out of the goat's pen?

1. After the man puts the trash in the trash can, what will he do?

2. Why are bags of trash put in cans?

Name: _____

Instructor's Worksheet

Directions: Before beginning, each student should be given a copy of the page that corresponds to the instructor's worksheet. The students are to look at each picture while the instructor reads the questions aloud. One student will answer each question (taking turns). The other students can be asked if they agree. If an answer needs to be expanded, the instructor should ask the child additional questions so that the final result is a logical answer.

1. After the baker makes the doughnuts, what do you think he will do?

2. Why do people like doughnuts so much?

1. After the children put frosting on the cake, what will they do?

2. Why does frosting get all over your fingers?

1. After the lady finishes washing the dishes, what will she do?

2. How do dishes get dirty?

1. After the boy puts the clean socks in the drawer, what will he do?

2. Why do socks need to be washed?

Name: _____

Instructor's Worksheet

Directions: Before beginning, each student should be given a copy of the page that corresponds to the instructor's worksheet. The students are to look at each picture while the instructor reads the questions aloud. One student answers a question (taking turns). The other students can be asked if they agree. If an answer needs to be expanded, the instructor should ask the child additional questions so that the final result is a logical answer.

1. After the construction worker finishes drinking his coffee, what should he do with his cup? Why?

2. How do you know he is up very high?

1. After the girl finishes her letter, what should she do? Why?

2. Why do people put stamps on letters?

1. If the man doesn't want his pants to burn with the hot iron, what should he do?

2. Why do people use hot irons to press clothes?

1. After the boy walks through the gate, what will he probably do?

2. Why do people put up fences around their yards?

Name: _____

Instructor's Worksheet

Directions: Before beginning, each student should be given a copy of the picture that corresponds to the instructor's worksheet. The students are to look at each picture while the instructor reads the questions aloud. One student answers a question (taking turns). The other students can be asked if they agree. If an answer needs to be expanded, the instructor should ask the child additional questions so that the final result is a logical answer.

1. If the girl wants to write a letter, what should she use?

2. Why do people use pens instead of of chalk to write letters?

1. If the girl wants to land on her feet, what should she quickly do?

2. What will happen if she doesn't drop her feet down?

1. If the boy does not want to cut his hand, what should he do?

2. Why does he turn the carving knife away from him when he carves?

1. If the boy wants the music to be very loud, what should he do?

2. If he wants the music to be soft, what should he do?

Instructor's Worksheet

Directions: Before beginning, each student should be given a copy of the page that corresponds to the instructor's worksheet. The students are to look at each picture while the instructor reads the questions aloud. One student will answer each question (taking turns). The other students can be asked if they agree. If an answer needs to be expanded, the instructor should ask the child additional questions so that the final result is a logical answer.

1. After the boy gets tucked in bed, what will he probably do?

2. Why do you think he will not be cold tonight?

1. If the boy needs a smooth place to skate, where should he skate?

2. If he hits a rock, what will probably happen?

1. If the umpire flips the coin and can't catch it, what will probably happen to the coin?

2. Why do umpires flip coins?

1. After the boy finishes taking his shower, what will he probably do?

2. How do you keep the water from being too hot?

Name: _____

Instructor's Worksheet

Directions: Before beginning, each student should be given a copy of the page that corresponds to the instructor's worksheet. The students are to look at each picture while the instructor reads the questions aloud. One student answers a question (taking turns). The other students can be asked if they agree. If an answer needs to be expanded, the instructor should ask the child additional questions so that the final result is a logical answer.

1. After the children finish eating, what will they probably do?

2. What will they do if it starts to rain?

1. What do you think the girl will do if she finds a dime?

2. How do people get money out of a piggy bank?

1. If the girl wants to know if it is dark outside, what should she do?

2. Why do people close the blinds at night?

1. Before the girl crosses the street, what should she do?

2. Why is it important to look both ways?

Name: _____

Instructor's Worksheet

Directions: Before beginning, each student should be given a copy of the page that corresponds to the instructor's worksheet. The students are to look at each picture while the instructor reads the questions aloud. One student answers a question (taking turns). The other students can be asked if they agree. If an answer needs to be expanded, the instructor should ask the child additional questions so that the final result is a logical answer.

1. After the artist gets his paintbrush, what will he do next?

2. Why do artists use paint palettes?

1. After the man splits the wood, what will he do with the wood?

2. Where do logs come from?

1. If the man wants the wallpaper to stay flat on the wall, what will he probably do?

2. What is put on the back side of the wallpaper to make it stick to the wall?

1. What should the man do if he does not know which lock the key fits?

2. Can you use a lock if it does not have a key?

Instructor's Worksheet

Directions: Before beginning, each student should be given a copy of the page that corresponds to the instructor's worksheet. The students are to look at each picture while the instructor reads the questions aloud. One student answers a question (taking turns). The other students can be asked if they agree. If an answer needs to be expanded, the instructor should ask the child additional questions so that the final result is a logical answer.

1. After the boys blow out the candles, what will they probably do?

2. Why do the candles need to be blown out?

1. After the baker rolls out the dough, what will he probably do?

2. Why is dough baked?

1. After the worker pushes the rocks in a pile, what will he probably do?

2. Why is heavy equipment needed to move rocks?

1. After the airplane lands, what will the passengers do?

2. Why do airplanes have wings?

Instructor's Worksheet

Directions: Before beginning, each student should be given a copy of the page that corresponds to the instructor's worksheet. The students are to look at each picture while the instructor reads the questions aloud. One student answers a question (taking turns). The other students can be asked if they agree. If an answer needs to be expanded, the instructor should ask the child additional questions so that the final result is a logical answer.

1. After she turns on the hairdryer, what should the beautician do?

2. Why don't people walk around with wet hair?

1. After the baseball player hits the ball, what should he do?

2. Why do baseball players wear gloves?

1. After the train stops, what will the engineer do?

2. Why does the train have an engineer?

1. The man picked up his hat off a table. What do you think he will do now?

2. Why do people wear hats?

Name: _____

Instructor's Worksheet

Directions: Before beginning, each student should be given a copy of the page that corresponds to the instructor's worksheet. The students are to look at each picture while the instructor reads the questions aloud. One student answers a question (taking turns). The other students can be asked if they agree. If an answer needs to be expanded, the instructor should ask the child additional questions so that the final result is a logical answer.

1. After the lady heats the soup, what will she do?

2. Why do people heat soup before eating it?

1. After the girl scrapes the food off the plate, what will she do?

2. Why is food scraped off the plate before it is washed?

1. After the man puts the money in the cash register, what will he do?

2. Why is it better to put money in a cash register instead of a basket?

1. After the bride puts on her wedding dress, what will she do?

2. Why do brides wear wedding dresses?

Instructor's Worksheet

Directions: Before beginning, each student should be given a copy of the page that corresponds to the instructor's worksheet. The students are to look at each picture while the instructor reads the questions aloud. One student answers a question (taking turns). The other students can be asked if they agree. If an answer needs to be expanded, the instructor should ask the child additional questions so that the final result is a logical answer.

1. After the pitcher has the ball in his hand, what will he do next?

2. Why does the catcher have on a mask?

1. If the lady wants to buy something from the bakery, what will she do?

2. Why do people buy bakery products instead of making them?

1. If the bus driver comes to a red light, what should he do?

2. Why is a bus so big and long?

1. After the man picks up his golf club, what will he do?

2. Why will he swing the club hard?

Instructor's Worksheet

Directions: Before beginning, each student should be given a copy of the page that corresponds to the instructor's worksheet. The students are to look at each picture while the instructor reads the questions aloud. One student answers a question (taking turns). The other students can be asked if they agree. If an answer needs to be expanded, the instructor should ask the child additional questions so that the final result is a logical answer.

1. After the man finishes cutting the grass, what do you think he will do?

2. Why does grass need to be cut so often?

1. After the girl opens the door and turns on the light, what do you think she will do?

2. Why do people put lights on at night before walking through rooms?

1. After the boy picks up the drum sticks, what do you think he will do?

2. Why do drums make so much noise?

1. After the man pulls up the carrot, what do you think he will do?

2. Why do carrots need to be pulled?

Instructor's Worksheet

The man is giving the clerk a dollar.

1. What do you think the clerk will do?

2. Why do people pay money for groceries?

The man wants to fasten the paper to the wall.

1. What do you think he will do?

2. How do thumbtacks stay in the wall?

The mother heard the baby crying.

1. What do you think she will do?

2. Why do babies usually cry?

The man picked up his camera.

1. What do you think he will do?

2. Why do cameras need film in them?

Name: _____

Instructor's Worksheet

1. After the man cuts the meat, what do you think he will probably do?

2. Why does he need a knife to cut the meat?

1. After the pitcher is full, what do you think the boy will do with the water?

2. Why do people have water faucets outside their houses?

1. After the fire is put out, what do you think the fireman will probably do?

2. Why do firemen put water on fires?

1. After the man is cool, what do you think he will do?

2. Why do people use fans?

Instructor's Worksheet

Directions: Before beginning, each student should be given a copy of the page that corresponds to the instructor's worksheet. The students are to look at each picture while the instructor reads the questions aloud. One student answers a question (taking turns). The other students can be asked if they agree. If an answer needs to be expanded, the instructor should ask the child additional questions so that the final result is a logical answer.

1. After the boy buys the candy, what do you think he will do?

2. Why do people love candy?

1. After the boy turns the door handle, what do you think he will do?

2. Why do doors have knobs?

1. After the man puts on his diving suit and equipment, what do you think he will do?

2. Why does he need this equipment when he goes under water?

1. After the man cooks the steak, what do you think he will do?

2. Why do people cook meat before they eat it?

Name: _____

Instructor's Worksheet

Directions: Before beginning, each student should be given a copy of the page that corresponds to the instructor's worksheet. The students are to look at each picture while the instructor reads the questions aloud. One student answers a question (taking turns). The other students can be asked if they agree. If an answer needs to be expanded, the instructor should ask the child additional questions so that the final result is a logical answer.

1. After the girl finishes taking a bath, what do you think she will do?

2. Why do people take baths?

1. After the girl catches the ball, what do you think she will do?

2. Why do you think they are tossing a big, round ball instead of a golf ball?

1. After the girl finishes coloring the picture, what do you think she will do?

2. Why are crayons kept in a box?

1. After the man puts ketchup on his hamburger, what do you think he will do?

2. Why do people put ketchup on hamburgers?

Instructor's Worksheet

Directions: Before beginning, each student should be given a copy of the page that corresponds to the instructor's worksheet. The students are to look at each picture while the instructor reads the questions aloud. One student answers a question (taking turns). The other students can be asked if they agree. If an answer needs to be expanded, the instructor should ask the child additional questions so that the final result is a logical answer.

1. After the boy gathers the logs, what do you think he will do with them?

2. Why do the logs need to be cut?

1. When the elevator doors open, what do you think the man will do?

2. Why do buildings need elevators?

1. After the man lights the match, what do you think he will do?

2. Why do people build fires in fireplaces?

1. After the boy puts glue on the paper, what do you think he will do?

2. Why does glue hold things together?

Instructor's Worksheet

<u>Directions:</u> Before beginning, each student should be given a copy of the page that corresponds to the instructor's worksheet. The students are to look at each picture while the instructor reads the questions aloud. One student answers a question (taking turns). The other students can be asked if they agree. If an answer needs to be expanded, the instructor should ask the child additional questions so that the final result is a logical answer.

1. After the man butters the bread, what do you think he will do?

2. What can people make out of slices of bread?

1. After the man gets his shears, what do you think he will do?

2. Why do shears have long blades?

1. After he snips off the man's hair, what do you think the barber will do?

2. What would people look like if they never cut their hair?

1. After the man unbuttons his shirt, what do you think he will do?

2. Why do shirts have buttons?

Instructor's Worksheet

Directions: Before beginning, each student should be given a copy of the page that corresponds to the instructor's worksheet. The students are to look at each picture while the instructor reads the questions aloud. One student answers a question (taking turns). The other students can be asked if they agree. If an answer needs to be expanded, the instructor should ask the child additional questions so that the final result is a logical answer.

1. If the little girl pats the baby chick too hard, what do you think will probably happen?

2. How do feathers help chickens?

1. If the boy lets go of the string, what do you think will happen?

2. How does the air stay in the balloon?

1. If the boy's umbrella leaks, what do you think will happen?

2. Why does an umbrella turn down instead of up?

1. If the car runs out of gas, what do you think will happen?

2. Why do cars have wheels?

Instructor's Worksheet

Directions: Before beginning, each student should be given a copy of the page that corresponds to the instructor's worksheet. The students are to look at each picture while the instructor reads the questions aloud. One student answers a question (taking turns). The other students can be asked if they agree. If an answer needs to be expanded, the instructor should ask the child additional questions so that the final result is a logical answer.

1. What do you think the mother will do if the baby drops the rattle?

2. Why do babies like to shake rattles?

1. The baby is sad. What do you think her mother will probably do?

2. Why do babies wear bibs?

1. After the glass is full, what do you think the girl will do?

2. Why does the pitcher have a spout?

1. She just kissed her mother good night. What do you think she will do now?

2. Why do people kiss each other?

Name: _____

Instructor's Worksheet

Directions: Before beginning, each student should be given a copy of the page that corresponds to the instructor's worksheet. The students are to look at each picture while the instructor reads the questions aloud. One student answers a question (taking turns). The other students can be asked if they agree. If an answer needs to be expanded, the instructor should ask the child additional questions so that the final result is a logical answer.

1. If it starts raining with thunder and lightning, what will the farmer, the horse and the cow probably do?

2. Why do you think barns have double doors?

1. After the boy washes his hands, what do you think he should do?

2. Why do people wash their hands with soap?

1. After the boy sweeps the dirt into the dustpan, what do you think he will do next?

2. What other ways can people get dirt off the floor?

1. After the boy puts money in the soda machine, what do you think will happen next?

2. Why do stores have drink machines?

Instructor's Worksheet

Directions: Before beginning, each student should be given a copy of the page that corresponds to the instructor's worksheet. The students are to look at each picture while the instructor reads the questions aloud. One student answers a question (taking turns). The other students can be asked if they agree. If an answer needs to be expanded, the instructor should ask the child additional questions so that the final result is a logical answer.

1. After the person buys a magazine, what do you think that person will probably do?

2. Why do people buy magazines?

1. Now that the man has his hammer, what do you think he will do?

2. Why do nails have sharp points?

1. After the children cook their marshmallows, what do you think they will do?

2. Why are they using sticks with sharp points?

1. Now that the girl has made snowballs, what do you think she will do?

2. Why does the girl need mittens?

Instructor's Worksheet

Directions: Before beginning, each student should be given a copy of the page that corresponds to the instructor's worksheet. The students are to look at each picture while the instructor reads the questions aloud. One student answers a question (taking turns). The other students can be asked if they agree. If an answer needs to be expanded, the instructor should ask the child additional questions so that the final result is a logical answer.

1. After the man cracks the nut, what do you think he will do?

2. Why is he using a nutcracker?

1. After the children finish the game, what do you think they will do?

2. Why do people roll the dice in the game?

1. After the nurse takes the little boy's temperature, what do you think she will do?

2. Why do people use thermometers?

1. After the man grabs his net, what do you think he will do?

2. Why does the net not hurt the butterfly?

Instructor's Worksheet

Directions: Before beginning, each student should be given a copy of the page that corresponds to the instructor's worksheet. The students are to look at each picture while the instructor reads the questions aloud. One student answers a question (taking turns). The other students can be asked if they agree. If an answer needs to be expanded, the instructor should ask the child additional questions so that the final result is a logical answer.

1. After the bear catches the fish, what do you think the bear will do?

2. How do bears catch fish?

1. After the dog begs for food, what do you think it will do?

2. How do dogs tell people they are hungry?

1. After the mother bird catches a worm, what do you think she will do?

2. Why do birds build their nests in trees?

1. After the beaver chops the tree, what do you think will happen?

2. How do beavers' flat tails help them?

Instructor's Worksheet

Directions: Before beginning, each student should be given a copy of the page that corresponds to the instructor's worksheet.   The students are to look at each picture while the instructor reads the questions aloud.   One student answers a question (taking turns).   The other students can be asked if they agree.   If an answer needs to be expanded, the instructor should ask the child additional questions so that the final result is a logical answer.

1. After the man opens his mouth, what do you think he will do?

2. Why do people have teeth?

1. Now that the farmer has his hoe, what do you think he will do?

2. How does digging around a plant help it?

1. After the man gets on his horse, what do you think he will do?

2. Why do people use saddles when they ride horses?

1. After the man puts gas in the lady's gas tank, what do you think the lady will do?

2. Why do people buy gas for their cars?

Name: _____

Instructor's Worksheet

1. After the boy rakes the leaves in a pile, what do you think he will probably do?

2. Why do rakes have prongs?

1. After the baker takes the cookies out of the oven, what do you think he will do?

2. Why must the baker be careful not to overbake the cookies?

1. What should the boy wear on his hand so that it does not hurt when he catches the ball?

2. How does a glove help protect a person's hand?

1. What do you think the boy will do when he takes the paper off the lollipop?

2. Why do lollipops have sticks?

Instructor's Worksheet

Directions: Before beginning, each student should be given a copy of the page that corresponds to the instructor's worksheet. The students are to look at each picture while the instructor reads the statement and questions aloud. One student answers a question (taking turns). The other students can be asked if they agree. If an answer needs to be expanded, the instructor should ask the child additional questions so that the final result is a logical answer.

The man pinned one end of the sheet to the clothesline.

1. What do you think he will do next?

2. What do clothespins do?

The little boy's mother told him not to eat the cupcake before dinner.

1. What do you think the boy will do?

2. Why would the cupcake spoil his appetite?

The boy took out his Halloween costume.

1. What do you think he will do next?

2. Why do children wear Halloween costumes?

The boy wants his bicycle to move.

1. What should the boy do next?

2. Why does a bicycle need handle-bars?

Instructor's Worksheet

Directions: Before beginning, each student should be given a copy of the page that corresponds to the instructor's worksheet. The students are to look at each picture while the instructor reads the statement and questions aloud. One student answers a question (taking turns). The other students can be asked if they agree. If an answer needs to be expanded, the instructor should ask the child additional questions so that the final result is a logical answer.

The boy wants to get off the swing.

1. What do you think he should do first?

2. Why must swings be tied to something strong?

The cowboy is whirling his rope in a circle.

1. What do you think he will do now?

2. How do cowboys use lassos?

The girl wants to learn to jump rope.

1. What do you think she will do?

2. Why does the rope have handles?

The man has his checkbook and a pen.

1. What do you think he will do next?

2. Why do people write checks?

Name: _____

Instructor's Worksheet

Directions: Before beginning, each student should be given a copy of the page that corresponds to the instructor's worksheet. The students are to look at each picture while the instructor reads the questions aloud. One student answers a question (taking turns). The other students can be asked if they agree. If an answer needs to be expanded, the instructor should ask the child additional questions so that the final result is a logical answer.

1. If the boy doesn't want his dog to be soapy, what will he do next?

2. Why do people wash their dogs?

1. After the girl takes off her coat, what should she do?

2. Why should coats be hung up?

1. If the girl wants a piece of pie, what should she do?

2. Why do pies have crusts?

1. After the girl takes the gift, what do you think she will do?

2. Why do people wrap presents?